<u>Prepare Yourself For Hypnosis</u>

- A Guide to Visualisation Mastery

By Laura Anne Whitworth

About the Author

Laura Anne Whitworth is a Quantum Healing Hypnosis Practitioner (QHHT®) trained in the hypnosis methods of the late, great Dolores Cannon. Laura is based in Chesterfield which is in Derbyshire in the United Kingdom. As well as practicing Quantum Healing for clients up and down the UK, Laura is also a fulltime Mother to two children. This work included, Laura is also the author of 'Isadora Stone and the Magic Portal' available on Amazon. This is a fiction book based on disclosure topics aimed at young adults.

Laura also has a YouTube channel where she discusses incredible information regarding the Ascension of Planet Earth that has been derived from Quantum Healing sessions. She also shares her latest opinions on the energies coming into the planet and disclosure topics.

You can find Laura online on her Laura Whitworth YouTube channel or alternatively on her Facebook page which is 'Quantum Healing Hypnosis Chesterfield with Laura Whitworth'.

Alternatively if you would like to book a Quantum Healing Hypnosis Session with Laura please email lauraanne.whitworth@gmail.com

Hypnosis

I absolutely love my job. It is the most rewarding job to be able to help people heal through finding out more about themselves. I see people walk into my office and they are so weary. Weary of life on this planet. Weary of battling illnesses that have taken over their life and mobility. Weary of the rat race and the constant pressure to conform to the 'norms' of society. They sit down in front of me and I feel their pain instantly. They are desperate for help. Desperate for healing. Desperate to be heard.

I am eternally grateful to the wonderful Dolores Cannon for devising her technique of hypnosis. I am also so thankful that Dolores has allowed her technique to be taught far and wide all over the Earth so we can as Practitioners keep helping people. Quantum Healing Hypnosis is an incredible healing modality and the changes and healing that I have personally witnessed through using this technique is extraordinary to say the least. It changes people's lives. It gives people their life and health back. It brings about such clarity and profound change that people upon completing a session are never the same again.

But what about the people who are unable to 'go under hypnosis'. Every so often I encounter a client who struggles to visualise. Any good hypnotherapist will tell you that the ability to visualise is key, particularly when undertaking past life regression.

About 10% of people will struggle to 'go into' the right side of the brain which is the place where the images are stored. Whilst this guide does not profess to be a miracle cure in terms of achieving the state necessary for hypnosis, it will provide you with a place to start in terms of training yourself to be able to visualise. Once you can visualise, you will be able to undertake a hypnosis session. Once you can visualise you will be able to 'see' your past lives and experience them as you have developed your inner vision. This guide is for people who have already undertaken a Hypnosis Session and have been unable to 'access the images' as they have not been able to see anything. It is also for people who are interested in undergoing a Hypnosis session but are worried that the hypnosis may not work for them as they struggle to visualise. If you work your way through the exercises in this book and make the necessary lifestyle changes, you will be well on your way to developing your inner vision.

This guide is also for people who are keen to try Hypnosis and want to ensure that their inner vision is up to speed before their session.

Diet

I cannot stress enough the importance that diet plays in being able to access your inner sight.

In the world that we live in our pineal glands have become calcified through the water that we drink which contains fluoride and the metals that are ingested by us daily.

Most of us are not even aware that we are supposed to be able to access this inner world within us, and that when we close our eyes and be still, it is normal to be able to see images play out in our 'mind's eye.'

We all need to have de-calcified pineal glands in order to be able to access our inner vision, and regardless of this as a goal, we should not be drinking water that is full of fluoride anyway as it is not good for our bodies.

The following are the changes that I would suggest as a way of getting the body ready for a Quantum Healing Hypnosis Session. They are also good lifestyle changes to make in general to ensure health and vitality.

- Drink good quality water daily that is fluoride free. You can achieve this through a water distiller or a good quality water filter. Mineral water is also a good quality water. If you are going to use a water distiller please also research what minerals you need to add in order to ensure that you are not lacking in minerals as the Distiller will take everything out including the good stuff!

- Eat food that contains 'Light'. By this I mean food that is grown from the Earth itself and not food that is light in terms of weight. The 'Light' that the food contains gives you additional life force and energy. Things that grow using the love from our Sun and the water from our Earth contain LIFE.
- Cook with Coconut Oil (Caprylic Acid)
- Cook with colourful vegetables and fruits flavoured with natural spices and herbs.
- Take a spoonful of Apple Cider Vinegar Daily.
- Take a spoonful of Coconut Oil Daily (Caprylic Acid). You can also 'pull' this oil through your teeth after brushing them as part of your daily routine and the oil is really good for your gums health.
- Take Probiotics to put back good bacteria in your gut.
- Add a slice of lemon to your water that you drink.
- Add Epsom salts to your daily bath.
- Diatomaceous Earth (Food Grade) is an excellent way of moving metals out of your body that are stored in the various tissues.
- If you can afford it, try and eat Organic Produce. You are directly ingesting the vibration of the food that you eat. You want to be eating food that has had a good life and is happy!

Also one thing that we can all do to raise the vibration of the food that we are about to eat and then in turn ourselves, is bless our food before we eat it. Give thanks for the sustenance that you are about to ingest it keeps you alive. Feel true gratitude. You are blessed to have food to eat.

Lifestyle changes

- Check your products that you use – Shampoo, Conditioner, Deodorants etc. and ensure that they are Aluminum free. You do not want Aluminum on your skin or in your body. It is this that makes its way to your Pineal Gland and calcifies it along with the Fluoride in your water and toothpaste.
- Invest in Fluoride free Toothpaste.
- Drink more water!
- Eat more good quality fruit and vegetables.
- Spend some time each day just relaxing with your eyes closed. Quieten the mind and just be. Listen to anything you hear and be aware of any images that you see.
- Get out in nature as often as possible and connect with your planet. We are all one. We are spending too much time out of step with our planet and the planets natural heartbeat and frequency. Go outside onto the grass. Take off your shoes and socks and Ground yourself and your energy into the planet. The Earth will adjust your frequency back in harmony with its own. You will instantly feel better if you do this!
- When you can, sit with your back against a tree and relax. Trees link directly into the heart of our planet and are all connected by the root system. Sitting with your back against a tree has the power to raise your vibration very quickly as your energy field is affected by the energy field of the tree.
- Every day when you wake up list all of the things in your life that you are grateful for. There is so much to be grateful for! When you plant your feet on the floor after waking up focus on the texture of the carpet and feel alive! Notice how good the water feels cascading down your skin in a morning as you get ready in the shower. Feel grateful for that shower! Some

people in their entire lives will never feel the glory of a hot shower. We are blessed! As you pour your morning coffee and eat your breakfast, savor it and feel gratitude. Also be present when you eat your food. Are you enjoying it? Does the food you are eating feel like it is full of vitality and is it raising your vibration? Or does it feel like it is lifeless? Do you need to be making better food choices in order to give you the energy that you need and deserve?

Relaxation

In our busy lives today we have forgotten how to relax. We are always taught 'time is money' 'the early bird catches the worm' 'no pain no gain' and a variety of other phrases parroted at us by well-meaning people encouraging us to constantly be on the run.

We have forgotten how to relax. We have forgotten how to close our eyes, be quiet and just be. It is when you are in this state of relaxation that your profoundest ideas will come to you. They will just drop in your head. As you have given them the space they need to arrive.

Our bodies are so used to being stressed and dashing from one place to another that we have forgotten how to listen to them.

We push our bodies until we sprain ankles, damage ligaments, rip muscles and suffer exhaustion.

We don't have time to face our emotions and because of this we manifest disease within our bodies.

We are encouraged to push ourselves to the limit in order to reach the heady heights of success, losing touch with the knowledge that success is already inside of you. And you have the power to manifest it. You hold everything you need for success inside of you and you can reach it through the power of visualization.

In order to slide into the Theta state which is required for hypnosis, you need to be able to relax. If you are a heavy coffee or tea drinker and are used to a lot of caffeine in your diet, I would strongly suggest gradually cutting back on the caffeine that you are ingesting in the lead up to your hypnosis session.

In the weeks leading up to your hypnosis session, carve out at least 15 minutes a day to just sit and relax and practice the following techniques. If you want to get the most out of your session it is of paramount importance that you are able to visualize.

Preparation

I would strongly suggest reading each visualisation exercise through before attempting to do it. As you will have to do the exercise from memory when you do it. You need to familiarize yourself with it first.

Also I would suggest you find a quiet place to do these exercises where you will not be disturbed.
I would also suggest having some food on hand to 'ground' you after practicing these exercises and if you own any crystals like Shungite or Black Tourmaline (or any of the dark ones) these will help you ground back into your body after too.

Visualisation Exercise 1

Dreams. This is where you start. All of us will dream at some point. And when you dream you are viewing images in the right side of the brain which is where we view images through the technique of hypnosis.

The first technique that I want you to start doing on a daily basis is writing down your dreams when you wake up. Do it as soon as you wake up as they will start to disappear very quickly. Doing this action of remembering your dreams, causes you to visualise what you are remembering so you are exercising the part of your brain that uses visualisation and you are developing your inner sight.

Start a dream diary and keep it for at least two weeks before your hypnosis session.

Write as much detail down as you can including the colours of things if you can remember them. Also any emotions that you experienced in people in your dreams, write these down too. Any sights and smells you can remember, write these down also. Any textures of things. Any places you saw. Any animals you encountered. Any loved ones, strangers, work colleagues! Write it all down on a daily basis.

Visualisation Exercise 2

In your dream journal (maybe in the back?) Write down your favourite memories that you have from your life so far.

Focus on how old you were and what you looked like. How you felt. What colours can you see whilst you revisit your memory? Who was there with you? What did they look like? Where were you? Were you out in nature? Inside or outside? Which country were you in? What was the weather like at the time? Can you remember being hot or cold? What emotions were you feeling when you revisit this memory. As you are revisiting the memory, focus on how you are 'seeing' it. Become aware of this. Really aware of this. As you revisit this memory, you are still aware that you are sat where you are in the room. But you can also 'see' and experience this memory. How are you doing it?

You are not physically seeing it with your eyes are you? You are seeing it with your 'mind's eye.' So what is the mind's eye? A lot of my clients struggle with this part the most. They struggle with seeing things through the 'mind's eye'.

It's there, but it's not there.

You can see it, but you can't see it.

You have to work at it to develop this kind of sight.

When you revisit this really fond memory of yours that you have, really, really focus on how it feels to 'see' it. Because how it feels to 'see' this memory will be exactly how it feels to 'see' your past lives during past life regression. This is the biggest piece of advice that I have to give people who want to undertake a Quantum Healing or Past Life Regression Session. People think due to the visual stimulation that we have of the TV these days that their past lives will play out before them like an action movie. It can feel very real like this when you are fully immersed in the life, but to start off with you will see a series of images that may appear and then withdraw. Just like you do when you try and recall a favourite memory of yours. Be aware of the difference of watching something on TV with your eyes. And how you see things when you watch a memory in your mind. The more you use this 'inner eye' the stronger it will become until you can actually have a scene or an image playing out in your inner eye whilst your physical eyes watch a totally different scene that is playing out in the reality that you are in. When your inner sight is strong you can be aware of both places at once and have your attention in both places at once. Your eyes in the world that we see on Earth and your 'inner eye' playing out a totally different scene inside yourself.

Visualisation Exercise 3

Close your eyes and remember your favourite memory from the heady days of summer as a child. What was your favourite thing to do outside? Can you remember the feel of the grass on your skin when you were a child and how exciting it felt to lay down on the grass and roll down a hill. Imagine a hill in your mind. Picture yourself as a child and what you were wearing. Lay down on the top of that hill. You can feel the sun beating down on your skin and it feels incredible. The birds are singing all around you and you can hear the sounds of children's laughter in the background. You laugh inside with glee as you realise what you are going to do. You are going to roll down that hill.

Ready?

1

2

3

GO!!!!!

Feel the exhilaration of excitement and the feel of the grass moving across different parts of your skin.

The grass smells so sweet.

The sky meets the grass meets the sky.

And all too soon – it is over.

Shall we do it again!

Practice this until you can see it all clearly.

Visualisation Exercise 4

Think about your favourite food. Why is it your favourite food? How do you feel when you eat that food? What country does the food come from? What comes to mind when you think of that country? When was the last time you ate your favourite food. Where were you at the time? Who were you with? Did you manage to eat it all? How much was left? Can you cook this food yourself? If so how do you cook it? What ingredients do you need?

I want you to visualize a massive steaming plate of this food which is your favourite.
Breathe in the smells of that food.
Breathe it right the way in.
Pick up your knife and fork and set up your first bite.
Imagine how it feels when you put that forkful of food in your mouth. Focus on the temperature of the food in your mouth. What is the texture of the food like? What does it feel like as you chew it? How long do you chew it for before you swallow it? What does it feel like as it travels down your throat and into your stomach?

I would suggest doing this one after you have eaten as otherwise you will be ravenous! ;-)

Visualisation Exercise 5

Think of your favourite colour. Why is it your favourite colour? What is it about this colour that you like? What things in nature are this colour? What do these things look like? What texture are they? Do you have any clothes in this favourite colour of yours? What do these clothes look like? What do you look like when you wear these clothes? How do you feel when you wear these clothes in your favourite colour? Is there any food that comes in this colour? Do you ever eat this food? What does it taste like? Is the flavor bitter or sweet? Does this food grow in the ground or is it manmade? How do they make this food?

Are there any flowers that come in this favourite colour of yours?

What do these flowers look like?

Where do these flowers normally grow?

What kind of insects like to land on these flowers?

What do the insects look like next to the flowers?

Whatever your favourite colour is, I now want you to focus on the opposite. What is the opposite colour on the spectrum to your favourite colour? Do you like this colour too? Picture this colour next to your favourite colour and think if there is anything that exists that has both these two colours in it.

When you are ready bring your attention back to your physical body and into the room.

Visualisation Exercise 6

What is your favourite thing to do when you have some free time? Do you like to paint? Listen to music? What is your favourite music? Is it singing or just instruments? Do you like to play sports or do you like to read?

Whatever your favourite past-time is I want you to recall a recent time when you have undertaken this activity.
Focus on why it is that you enjoy it?
What do you feel when you do this activity?
What do you see when you do this activity?
If you were to associate a colour with this activity, what would it be and why?
Imagine yourself undertaking this activity now and really focus on why it is your favourite past-time.
What does it give you?
When you are ready bring your attention back to your physical body and back in the room.

Visualisation Exercise 7

Picture your favourite animal. When was the first time that you saw this animal in real life? How old were you? Focus on the colour of this animal. Is the animal your favourite colour or a different one? Does this animal normally socialise or does it prefer to be alone? If it socialises do all these animals look the same or is there some variation in their colourings? What do the babies of this animal look like? What is the normal habitat of this animal? Do they live on land or in the water? In the jungle or desert or are they a house animal? Picture your favourite animal in its natural habitat having fun and playing.

Now I want you to imagine that you are the animal. How does it feel to be behind the eyes of this animal when it is running? How does it feel to be this animal when it is laying in the sun grooming itself or sun gazing?

Now in your mind as this animal, I want you to begin to run. How does it feel to run as this animal? Exhilarating? Is this animal nearer to the floor than you are or higher from the floor?
Now I want you still as this animal in your mind, to walk up to the water in the habitat that it is in and drink some water.
How does it feel to drink water as this animal?
What would this animal eat?
And finally say goodbye to the animal and return your full focus to your own physical body.
After you have undertaken this exercise focus on how that made you feel. Did you find it easy to imagine yourself as the animal or hard? Practice this until you can be the animal easily.

Visualisation Exercise 8

What is your favourite place in the world to go? Examine within yourself why it is your favourite place. Is it the sights the smells? What are these sights and smells? Is it the architecture? The history? The nature? The paintings? The Sea? The Beach? Wherever this favourite place is of yours, I want you to put yourself there now.

Put yourself right there in the middle of your favourite place.
Focus on the sounds. What can you hear?
Focus on the colours. What colours can you see in this place?
What textures can you see?
How many people are there?
Is it just you?
Who are you with?
What are you doing?
How does it feel?
Bring your awareness to what it is about this place that you love so much.
Why has it become your favourite?
What is it that draws you so?
Spend some time in your favourite place.
And when you have finished gradually bring your awareness back into your body. Focus on your breathing and retain the lovely feeling that you felt of being in your favourite place.

Visualisation Exercise 9

I want you to imagine running a bath. (Don't really do this. You are imagining it!)

Picture your bathroom and walking into it and up to your bath.

See your hand putting the plug in your bath. Then turn the hot tap on. And the cold tap too if you don't like the bath too hot.

What do you put in the bath next? Do you use a drop of essential oil or Epsom salts? Do you use bubble bath or a bath bomb? Whatever you like to use drop it in the bath now.

See it start to fizz or bubble. What noise does that make?

How loud is the sound of the water as it hits the bottom of your bath? Does it hurt your ears or do you find the sound OK?

The bath is almost run now so after removing your clothes I want you to slowly and safely lower yourself into your imaginary bath.

Feel the biting sensation of the water as you lower yourself in as the water is slightly too hot. But you know within a few minutes it won't feel too hot at all. Lower yourself in and relax.

Feel the sensation of the water on your skin. Turn off the taps.

Allow all of your tension that you have collected throughout the day to just melt away into that bath water. Allow the water to take the stress for you. Imagine the water is full of light energy and as you are immersed in this bath, the water is giving light energy back to your body and revitalizing it. You stay in this bath for another minute and every second that ticks by you feel better and better and more alive. Now slowly and safely pull yourself up out of your imaginary bath and pull a nice warm fluffy towel off the radiator to dry yourself with. Focus on the sensation on that towel against your skin. Now slowly bring your focus back to your own physical body and back into the room.

Visualisation Exercise 10

I want you to imagine yourself walking up to a favourite beach that you have been to in your life before.

As you get closer to this beach you see that it is in fact deserted. There is only you on it.

You can hear the sounds of the waves gently lapping up against the sand. The constant rhythm of this is soothing and you find a sun lounger and place your towel on it.

Then you lower yourself down onto your sun lounger.

As you look out at the sea you open a bag that you have brought with you and take out a bottle of sun cream.

You start to open the sun cream but the top of the tube sticks and you have to really pull it hard to get it open. It makes a creaking sound.

You then squirt out a huge blob of cream and start rubbing the cream into your body.

Focus on the sensation of rubbing the cream into your body. Make sure you do every part of your body, including your ears and even between your toes.

Then lie back on the sun lounger and feel the sun beating down on your body.

The sun is the perfect temperature not too hot it burns, but you can feel its effect on your skin and it is lovely.

Focus on the pleasure of the sun on your skin and the sounds of the sea lapping against the sandy shore. When you are ready, bring your attention back to your physical body and into the room.

Visualisation Exercise 11

I want you to picture a forest.

It is the most beautiful forest you have ever seen.

You can't quite believe how green the trees are. They are so green it almost hurts your eyes.

As you walk through this forest on a meandering path, you suddenly hear the sounds of a distant stream.

You are so hot as you have been walking for a while and you are longing to take off your shoes and socks and put your feet into the cold stream.

Suddenly as you turn a corner you see the stream.

You race up to it and sit down on the bank of the stream and begin to undo the laces on your training shoes.

As you take your feet out of your shoes you are aware of how hot your feet have become walking they are almost steaming.

You peel off your sticky socks and plunge your aching feet into the cool crisp water and sigh a sigh of sheer bliss.

The water is heaven. It is so cold on this hot summers day.

As you sink your toes into the river bed floor, your toes touch the shiny smooth pebbles below the surface.

You can see the light from the sun dancing on the surface of the river and your toes wiggling on top of the pebbles below.

Stay in the stream as long as you want and when you are ready pull your awareness back to your physical body and back into the room.

Visualisation Exercise 12

You are in a beautiful meadow on a sunny day.

There is a gentle breeze blowing and it caresses your skin.

As you walk along a bee wafts past your face and you resist your initial reaction to swat it and wish it well on its busy way.

You watch the butterflies as they dance from flower to flower and are mesmerised by the vivid colours and patterns that the butterflies display on their delicate wings.

You decide to sit down in the middle of the meadow and just relax to pass the time.

As you lay down and your perspective changes, you look up at the sky.

It is the bluest you have ever seen it.

So very blue.

It almost shimmers.

A flock of birds flies into the sky that you are watching.

They dance before your eyes in a beautiful pattern that ebbs and flows.

As you lay in this meadow of complete peace, relax a while and see what thoughts come to you.

When you are ready to leave the meadow bring your awareness back to your physical body and back into the room.

Visualisation Exercise 13

It is winter and you are out in the snow having a snowball fight with a group of your favourite friends.

You have huge gloves on to protect your fingers but even so you can still feel the bite of winter.

You have made a stack of snowballs and are just about to throw them at your friends.

Just as you pick up the first snowball you feel a gentle thud on your back and you laugh. The snowball does not hurt as you have so many layers of clothes on in order to not feel too cold.

You laugh with your friends and throw snowballs at each other.

Once the snowballs have gone you decide to make a snowman.

You all work together to make the body, then the head.

One of you runs off to fetch a hat and some gloves for the snowman and some stones for its eyes and buttons.

All you need now is something for a nose.

You suddenly see a stick on the ground and you pick it up and place it in the centre of the snowman's face

The snowman looks so happy!

Even though it is so cold outside you are all so hot now after all the fun you have had.

You all go back inside and take off your coats and warm your hands.

You drink some nice warm hot chocolate and focus on the sweetness of the liquid as it runs down your throat and warms up your tummy.

When you are ready to come back bring your attention back to your physical body and back into the room.

Visualisation Exercise 14

You are stood on the top of a really tall mountain.

It is so tall that clouds are hanging just above your head in wispy white tendrils.

There is a smattering of snow on the top of this mountain where you stand, but as you look down the mountain, all you can see is Green. Green as far as the eye can see. Green fields, Green Trees, Green Mountain.

As you focus further on the mountain, you can see what look like different coloured ants crawling up the mountain. As you focus further still you realise that these 'ants' are people who are just starting out on their journey of scaling this huge mountain, and you feel a sense of pride that you have done it and you are at the top.

Suddenly you become aware of a figure approaching you.

Climbing up and over the top of the mountain and through the mist towards you.

You cannot believe your eyes when you see who it is.

Joy and happiness swells up in your chest.

You have really missed this person.

And as they walk closer to you, you can smell their familiar scent

Spend as long as you like with this special person, and when you are ready, bring your full awareness back to your physical body and back into the room.

And Finally...

When you can do all of these Visualisations from start to finish, and see everything in your mind's eye, you are ready for a hypnosis session.

Don't worry if you can't hear the noises or smell the smells, this will come with time. But if you can see the Visualisations then you are ready.

Start with the easier ones and master them first.

Once you can easily 'see' Visualisation Exercise 12, 13 and 14 you are ready!

And remember Hypnosis is not anesthesia!

You will be fully present the entire time you are under hypnosis. You will be aware of your physical body. You will be aware that your toe is itching, that your stomach is rumbling, that you need to use the bathroom etc. But whilst you are also aware of all these things about your physical body here, you will also be able to fully experience your past lives playing out in your mind's eye too - just like in these Visualisation Exercises.

Hypnosis is deep relaxation of the body with an alert and focused mind through visualisation. That is all. You are in complete control all the time and can stop the session whenever you want.

You can do this!

So practice, practice, practice and when you are ready, Go for it!

Much Love and happy Visualising!

Laura Whitworth

Printed in Great Britain
by Amazon